PRESIDENT ADAMS' ALLIGATOR
and Other White House Pets

Written and Illustrated by
Peter W. Barnes and
Cheryl Shaw Barnes

Edited by Betty Shepard and Lisa Pinnell

Other books by Peter and Cheryl Barnes

Woodrow, the White House Mouse, about the presidency and the nation's most famous mansion.
House Mouse, Senate Mouse, about Congress and the legislative process.
Marshall, the Courthouse Mouse, about the Supreme Court and the judicial process.
A "Mice" Way to Learn About Government, a teacher's curriculum guide for the three books above.
Capital Cooking with Woodrow and Friends, a cookbook for kids that mixes fun recipes with fun facts about
   American history and government.
Woodrow for President, about how Woodrow got to the White House.
A "Mice" Way to Learn About Voting, Campaigns and Elections, a teacher's curriculum guide for *Woodrow for
   President.*
Alexander, the Old Town Mouse, about historic Old Town, Alexandria, Va., across the Potomac River from
   Washington, D.C.
Nat, Nat, the Nantucket Cat (with Susan Arciero), about beautiful Nantucket Island, Mass.
Nat, Nat, the Nantucket Cat Goes to the Beach (with Susan Arciero), about a trip to the beach on Nat's favorite
   island.
Martha's Vineyard (with Susan Arciero), about wonderful Martha's Vineyard, Mass.
Cornelius Vandermouse, the Pride of Newport (with Susan Arciero), about historic Newport, R.I., home to
   America's most magnificent mansion houses.

Order these books through your local bookstore by title,
or order **autographed copies** of the Barnes's books by calling **1-800-441-1949** or from our website at
www.VSPBooks.com.

For a brochure and ordering information, write to:

VSP Books
P.O. Box 17011
Alexandria, VA 22302

To get on the mailing list, send your name and address to the address above.

Copyright © 2003 by Peter W. Barnes and Cheryl Shaw Barnes

ISBN 1-893622-13-4

Library of Congress Catalog Card Number: 2003096386

10 9 8 7 6 5 4 3 2 1

Printed in the United States of America

*This book is dedicated to the memory
of our father, Charles Stephen Shaw,
who was always our biggest fan.
We miss you, Dad!*

*We also want to thank our colleagues at VSP Books
for their hard work and enthusiasm day in and day out:
CeCe Iroma and Buddy and Barbara Miller. You are the best!*

—P.W.B and C.S.B.

Look for President Adams' alligator hidden in every illustration in this book.

Acknowledgments

*The idea for this book came when Cheryl was asked to illustrate the
2002 White House Christmas program for children. The theme was
"All Creatures Great and Small" and featured many White House
pets. We wish to thank First Lady Laura Bush and members of her
staff, including Clare Pritchett and Cathy Fenton, for their support
and encouragement in creating the program.*

"What is your favorite pet?" Mrs. Tucker asked her class.

All the children answered at once: "A mouse!" "My kitty!" "A big snake!" "Ewww!" "My guinea pig!" "A pony!" "My dog, Juno!"

"Wow, those all sound like great pets," Mrs. Tucker said. She noticed Billy in the back of the room doodling on some paper. "Billy? I didn't hear from you. Don't you have a favorite pet?"

Billy looked up and smiled. "I am drawing my favorite pet."

"Well, what is it?" Mrs. Tucker asked.

Billy picked up his picture and pointed to a bright green alligator with a big toothy grin.

"An alligator?!?" the kids screamed all at once. "An alligator isn't a pet!"

"Now hold on a second, class," Mrs. Tucker said. "An alligator can be a pet. Why, even one of our presidents had an alligator. In fact, the presidents had all kinds of pets—lots of dogs and cats, of course. But they also had some very strange pets."

"Like what?" the children asked.

"Why don't I tell you some stories about them. Then at the end of class, each of you can vote for your favorite presidential pet. How does that sound?"

"Great!" yelled the children.

"Our Founding Fathers loved animals. Did you know that our very first president, George Washington, had hunting dogs named Madame Moose, Sweetlips and Tipsy? He also had many horses. His favorite was a big, strong horse named Nelson. President Washington wanted to make sure all his horses had nice, healthy teeth, so he had them brushed regularly. You would need a pretty big toothbrush for that job! Our second president, John Adams, loved horses too. He loved one horse so much that he had a stable built for her right on the White House lawn. Her name was Cleopatra.

"Our third president, Thomas Jefferson, had two pet grizzly bears! He also had a pet mockingbird named Dick. The president and Dick were very close. Jefferson would let Dick sit on his shoulder and eat food from his lips! Dick also liked to sing along when the president played his violin. Another bird in the White House was Polly. Polly parrot was the pet of our fourth president, James Madison. President Madison also had a sheepdog.

"Clippety-clop, clippety-clop. Here come the presidents and their horses marching down the street to the sound of a beating drum. Everyone loves to show off his or her favorite pet. And what better way to show off a horse than in a parade? Andrew Jackson had horses named Sam Patches, Emily and Lady Bolivia. He loved these horses, but his favorite pet was a parrot named Poll. President William Henry Harrison brought his cow, Sukey, with him to the White House.

"President John Tyler rode a horse named The General and had two Italian wolfhounds. Zachary Taylor's favorite horse, Old Whitey, liked to snack on the grass of the White House lawn. Poor Old Whitey didn't have a very thick tail—visitors would sometimes pull out the hairs for souvenirs!

"Did you know that an alligator once lived in the White House? Back in 1825, a man named General Lafayette brought an alligator to live with President John Quincy Adams for a while. The president didn't know what to do with the alligator, so he put it in a bathtub in the East Room. Visitors and workers at the White House got a little scared when they wandered in and found a big green alligator splashing around in the tub. What would you do if you had an alligator in your bathtub?

"Sometimes presidents were given pets they could not keep in the White House. Martin Van Buren received two tiger cubs from the ruler of a foreign country. President Van Buren really wanted to keep the tiger cubs with him, but Congress decided they would have much more fun at the zoo. President James Buchanan was given lots of pets as presents. You see, Buchanan was the only president who never got married. So people thought lots of pets would help keep him company. A king gave him a whole herd of elephants, but Buchanan decided they should live at the zoo. Buchanan also had a pair of bald eagles that he kept at his farm. Buchanan's favorite pet was Lara, a very big dog known as a Newfoundland.

"Abraham Lincoln loved all kinds of animals. When he became president, he got many pets for his children, including ponies, rabbits and a turkey named Jack. Jack was supposed to be Christmas dinner, but Lincoln's son Tad fell in love with him and begged his dad to let him live. Of course, Lincoln could not say no—he loved animals as much as anyone.

"Lincoln also gave Tad two goats named Nanny and Nanko. One day, Tad tied Nanny and Nanko to a kitchen chair and raced through the halls of the White House. Mrs. Lincoln was having a tea party in the East Room when Tad burst in with the goats! President Lincoln tried hard not to laugh, but Mrs. Lincoln did not think it was very funny.

"Many presidents had egg-rolling parties at Easter. Sometimes their pets were included in the fun. Andrew Johnson brought two cows with him to the White House when he became president. He also left food out some nights for a family of mice. Ulysses S. Grant had a favorite horse named Butcher Boy and his daughter, Nellie, had one named Jennie.

"Benjamin Harrison had a frisky goat named Old Whiskers, who would pull his grandchildren around in a cart. One day Old Whiskers took off running with President Harrison's grandchildren in the cart. Harrison and his dog, Dash, had to run very fast to catch them. Rutherford B. Hayes and his wife, Lucy, had many pets, including a goat, canaries, dogs, kittens and a mockingbird. They made the egg roll an official event at the White House every Easter.

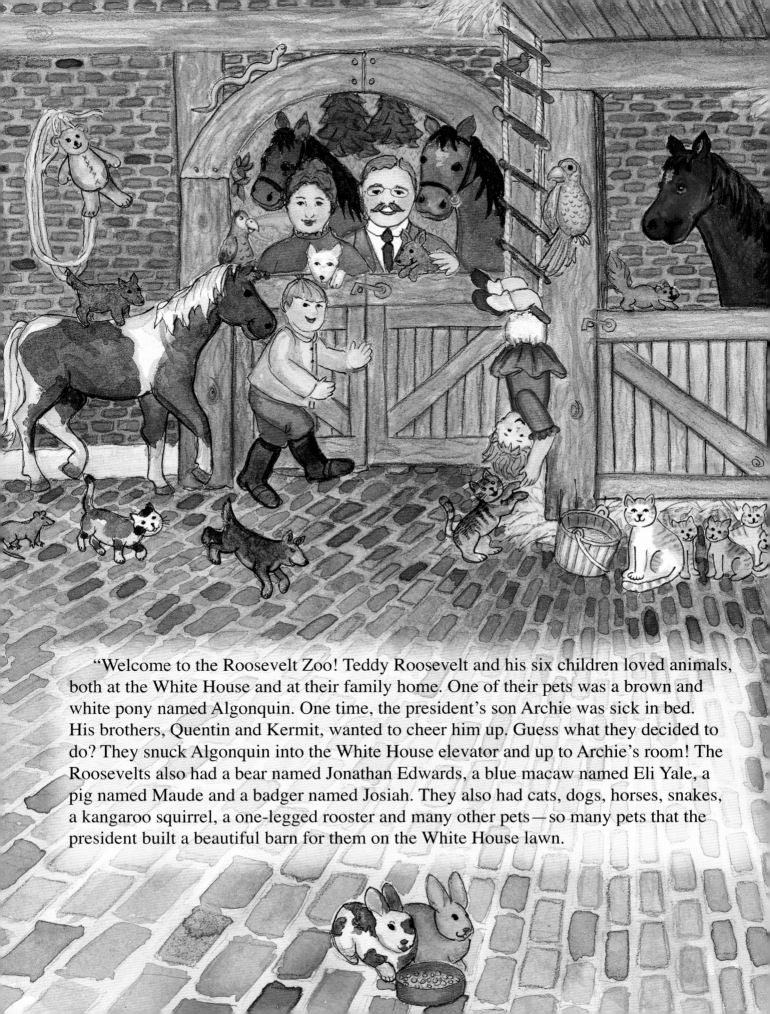

"Welcome to the Roosevelt Zoo! Teddy Roosevelt and his six children loved animals, both at the White House and at their family home. One of their pets was a brown and white pony named Algonquin. One time, the president's son Archie was sick in bed. His brothers, Quentin and Kermit, wanted to cheer him up. Guess what they decided to do? They snuck Algonquin into the White House elevator and up to Archie's room! The Roosevelts also had a bear named Jonathan Edwards, a blue macaw named Eli Yale, a pig named Maude and a badger named Josiah. They also had cats, dogs, horses, snakes, a kangaroo squirrel, a one-legged rooster and many other pets—so many pets that the president built a beautiful barn for them on the White House lawn.

"'Happy Birthday, Laddie Boy!' Laddie Boy was the favorite dog of President Warren Harding. Harding spoiled him terribly; he even threw Laddie Boy a birthday party with a cake made of dog biscuits covered in white icing.

"When Woodrow Wilson was president, he let his sheep graze on the White House lawn. They kept the lawn mowed by eating the grass until it was nice and short. One of them was named Old Ike, who became famous for chewing tobacco. William Howard Taft owned the last cow that lived in the White House. Its name was Pauline Wayne.

"Time for dinner with the Coolidges and their pets! Calvin Coolidge and his wife, Grace, almost had too many pets to count. They often ate in the dining room surrounded by their many animals. When the president yelled 'supper,' the dogs came running. They gave their dogs funny names like Calamity Jane, Tiny Tim and Boston Beans. Grace made elegant floppy hats trimmed with ribbons for their prissy white collie, Prudence Prim, to wear on special occasions.

"The president and Grace also had cats, birds, a donkey, a bobcat, a bear, a wallaby, two lion cubs and a pigmy hippo. Many of these animals had to live at the zoo because they were a little too wild for the White House. Grace hated to keep her birds in a cage so she let them fly around the White House. One bird even sat on the head of a maid as she did her housework! Coolidge's favorite pet was a raccoon named Rebecca. Coolidge would put a leash on Rebecca and walk her all around the White House.

"Dogs have always been popular pets with presidents. Some presidents' dogs were not very well behaved. Some were so bad they needed to go to obedience school! One of Franklin Roosevelt's dogs, Meg, bit a newspaper reporter on the nose. Another dog named Wink liked to steal bacon from peoples' breakfast plates.

"Roosevelt's German shepherd, Major, sometimes bit people. He once ripped the pants of a foreign leader visiting the White House. Roosevelt's favorite pet was a well-behaved dog named Fala. Fala was a Scottish terrier who became very famous. President Roosevelt took him everywhere, even on trips around the world.

"Time to play at the White House! John F. Kennedy and his wife, Jackie, had many dogs, including a famous one named Pushinka, who came from Russia. Mrs. Kennedy loved animals, especially horses, and so did her daughter, Caroline. Caroline's favorite pony, named Macaroni, wandered all around the White House lawn. Lyndon B. Johnson and his family had many beagles. Two of them were named Him and Her. His favorite dog was Yuki, a mutt from Texas who loved to howl.

"Dwight Eisenhower could have used a howling dog like Yuki. Eisenhower liked to practice golf on the White House lawn. Unfortunately, he had lots of problems with squirrels digging holes in his putting green. Without a dog like Yuki to howl and scare the squirrels away, they kept digging until finally they all had to be captured and taken to a park.

"Welcome home, Mr. President! Recent presidents travel in a helicopter called Marine One. Sometimes their pets are there to meet them when they return to the White House. Ronald Reagan had a little spaniel named Rex that would run to meet him and his wife, Nancy, as soon as they landed. President Reagan loved horses; he had five of them. He also had a sheepdog named Lucky that was so big and strong it looked like Mrs. Reagan was water skiing as Lucky dragged her when she tried to walk him.

"Richard Nixon had Vicky, a poodle; Pasha, a tiny Yorkshire terrier, and King Timahoe, an Irish terrier that liked to shake the hands of people who came to the White House. Gerald Ford had a Siamese cat named Chan and a golden retriever named Liberty, who had eight puppies. Jimmy Carter also had a Siamese cat. Its name was Misty Malarkey Ying Yang. He also had a dog named Grits.

"Let's play catch in the Rose Garden! Presidents George H.W. Bush and his son George W. are both dog lovers. The Bush family loves Springer spaniels, including one named Millie, who had six puppies. One of the puppies, Spotty, was given to George W., who also has a Scottish terrier, Barney, and a black cat named Willie. President Bill Clinton and his wife, Hillary, had a dog named Buddy. They also owned a famous cat, Socks, who loved to greet White House visitors.

"Wow! Can you believe all the different White House pets the presidents have had over the years? There were dogs, cats, birds, bears, cows, goats, horses and even an alligator! Which White House pet is your favorite? You can use your ballot to vote and tell why you like this pet the most. There are so many fun pets to choose from!"

Vote for Your Favorite White House Pet

Use this ballot to vote for your favorite one and explain why you like this pet the most.

_____

_____

_____

_____

_____

_____

_____

_____

_____

_____

_____

_____

_____

_____

_____

Bibliography

Bausum, Ann. *Our Country's Presidents*. Washington: National Geographic Society, 2001.

Blue, Rose, and Corine J. Naden. *The White House Kids*. Brookfield: The Millbrook Press, 1995.

Bowman, John. *The History of the American Presidency*. Rev. ed. North Dighton: World Publications Group, 2002.

Kelly, Niall. *Presidential Pets*. New York: Abbeville Press, 1992.

Kunhardt, Philip B., Jr., Philip B. Kunhardt III and Peter W. Kunhardt. *The American President*. New York: Riverhead Books, 1999.

Leiner, Katherine. *First Children: Growing Up in the White House*. New York: Tambourine Books, 1996.

Rowan, Roy, and Brooke Janis. *First Dogs: American Presidents and Their Best Friends*. Chapel Hill: Algonquin Books of Chapel Hill, 1997.

Seale, William. *The President's House*. 2 vols. Washington: White House Historical Association, 1986.

Truman, Margaret. *White House Pets*. New York: David McKay Company Inc., 1969.